# ARKANSAS

Explore the United States

**Sarah Tieck**

Big Buddy BOOKS
Explore the United States

## VISIT US AT
**www.abdopublishing.com**

Published by ABDO Publishing Company, PO Box 398166, Minneapolis, MN 55439.

Printed in the United States of America, North Mankato, Minnesota.
022012
092012

 PRINTED ON RECYCLED PAPER

Coordinating Series Editor: Rochelle Baltzer
Contributing Editors: BreAnn Rumsch, Marcia Zappa
Graphic Design: Adam Craven
Cover Photograph: *iStockphoto*: ©iStockphoto.com/dlewis33.
Interior Photographs/Illustrations: *Alamy*: Jeff Greenberg (p. 27); *AP Photo*: Charlotte Observer, Maureen A. Coyle (p. 25), Danny Johnston (p. 26), Carolyn Kaster (p. 23), Mark Lennihan (p. 25); *Getty Images*: Archive Photos (p. 13), Ed Lallo/Photolibrary (p. 19), William C. Shrout/Time Life Pictures (p. 13); *iStockphoto*: ©iStockphoto.com/Caitlin_Mirra (p. 27), ©iStockphoto.com/Davel5957 (p. 9), ©iStockphoto.com/dlewis33 (p. 21); *Shutterstock*: Natalia Bratslavsky (pp. 9, 11), Steve Byland (p. 30), Bonita R. Cheshier (p. 30), Ross Ellet (p. 17), Phillip Lange (p. 30), S R Mendez (p. 5), Caitlin Mirra (pp. 17, 26), Jason L. Price (p. 27), Clint Spencer (p. 29), Mary Terriberry (p. 30).

All population figures taken from the 2010 US census.

## Library of Congress Cataloging-in-Publication Data

Tieck, Sarah, 1976-
 Arkansas / Sarah Tieck.
   p. cm. -- (Explore the United States)
 ISBN 978-1-61783-342-7
 1. Arkansas--Juvenile literature. I. Title.
 F411.3.T54 2012
 976.7--dc23
                              2012000753

# ARKANSAS

# Contents

# ONE NATION

The United States is a **diverse** country. It has farmland, cities, coasts, and mountains. Its people come from many different backgrounds. And, its history covers more than 200 years.

Today, the country includes 50 states. Arkansas is one of these states. Let's learn more about Arkansas and its story!

### Did You Know?

Arkansas became a state on June 15, 1836. It was the twenty-fifth state to join the nation.

Land features in Arkansas include the Buffalo
National River (*above*) and the Ozark Mountains.

# ARKANSAS UP CLOSE

The United States has four main **regions**. Arkansas is in the South.

Arkansas has six states on its borders. Missouri is north. Oklahoma and Texas are west. Louisiana is south. And, Tennessee and Mississippi are east.

Arkansas has a total area of 53,179 square miles (137,733 sq km). About 3 million people live there.

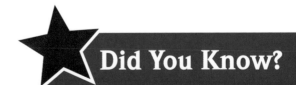

### Did You Know?

Washington DC is the US capital city. Puerto Rico is a US commonwealth. This means it is governed by its own people.

# REGIONS OF THE UNITED STATES

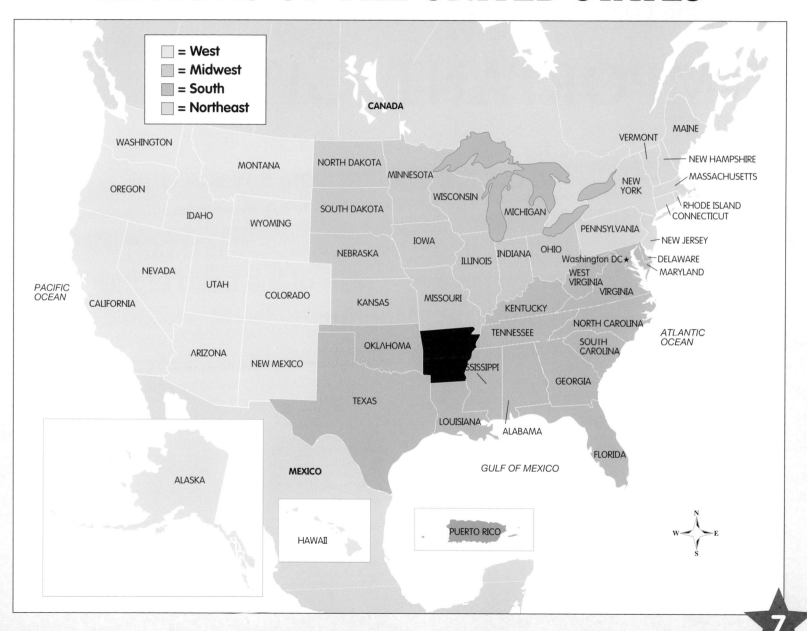

**Legend:**
- = West
- = Midwest
- = South
- = Northeast

CANADA

WASHINGTON

MONTANA

OREGON

IDAHO

WYOMING

NORTH DAKOTA

MINNESOTA

SOUTH DAKOTA

WISCONSIN

MICHIGAN

VERMONT

MAINE

NEW HAMPSHIRE

MASSACHUSETTS

NEW YORK

RHODE ISLAND
CONNECTICUT

PENNSYLVANIA

NEW JERSEY

NEVADA

UTAH

COLORADO

NEBRASKA

IOWA

ILLINOIS

INDIANA

OHIO

Washington DC ★

DELAWARE
MARYLAND

WEST VIRGINIA

VIRGINIA

PACIFIC OCEAN

CALIFORNIA

KANSAS

MISSOURI

KENTUCKY

NORTH CAROLINA

ATLANTIC OCEAN

ARIZONA

NEW MEXICO

OKLAHOMA

TENNESSEE

SOUTH CAROLINA

MISSISSIPPI

GEORGIA

TEXAS

LOUISIANA

ALABAMA

FLORIDA

GULF OF MEXICO

ALASKA

MEXICO

HAWAII

PUERTO RICO

N
W E
S

**7**

# Important Cities

Little Rock is the **capital** of Arkansas. It is also the state's largest city. It is home to 193,524 people.

Little Rock is in the middle of Arkansas. It is a port city on the Arkansas River. It is also at the base of the Ouachita (WAH-shuh-taw) Mountains.

The Arkansas River makes Little Rock important to business. Ships stop there to drop off and pick up goods.

The Arkansas State Capitol was built to look like the US Capitol. It has been used in movies as a stand-in.

## ARKANSAS

- Fayetteville
- Fort Smith
- ★ Little Rock

N W E S

9

Fort Smith is the second-largest city in Arkansas. It has 86,209 people. Fort Smith is on the western side of the state.

Fayetteville has 73,580 people. It is the third-largest city. People vacation there and visit the Ozark Mountains.

The University of Arkansas is in Fayetteville. Its Old Main clock tower is a well-known sight.

11

# ARKANSAS IN HISTORY

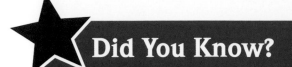
The history of Arkansas includes European explorers and the **Louisiana Purchase**. In 1541, Spanish explorer Hernando de Soto was the first European in Arkansas. Native Americans had lived there for thousands of years.

In 1673, the French began exploring and settling the land. In 1803, the United States bought a large piece of land from France. This was called the Louisiana Purchase. The land included Arkansas.

People celebrated the Louisiana Purchase. They raised the American flag and shot guns into the air.

De Soto was one of the first Europeans to explore North America. He was looking for gold.

# Timeline

**1842**

**1836**

**1868**

Arkansas became the twenty-fifth state on June 15.

The Old State House was completed in Little Rock.

Arkansas rejoined the United States.

1800s

President Thomas Jefferson bought land from France in the **Louisiana Purchase**. This included Arkansas.

Arkansas left the United States. It joined the Southern states to fight in the **American Civil War**.

**1803**

**1861**

**1932**

Hattie Caraway became the first female elected to the US Senate. She represented Arkansas until 1945.

**2004**

The William J. Clinton Presidential Library and Museum opened in Little Rock.

**2011**

Arkansas honored the 150th anniversary of the start of the **American Civil War**.

1900s

2000s

Oil was discovered near El Dorado. This natural **resource** changed business in Arkansas.

**1921**

Former Arkansas governor Bill Clinton was elected US president.

**1992**

Former Arkansas first lady Hillary Rodham Clinton ran for US president. She lost, but was named US secretary of state in 2009.

**2008**

15

# ACROSS THE LAND

Arkansas has rivers, forests, and mountains. The Mississippi River flows along the state's eastern border. The Arkansas River flows across the state. The Ozark and Ouachita Mountains cover part of Arkansas.

Many types of animals make their homes in Arkansas. Some of these include black bears, woodchucks, opossums, and catfish.

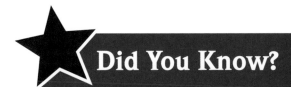

## Did You Know?

In July, the temperature in Little Rock ranges from about 70° to 90°F (20° to 30°C) in a day. In January, it ranges from about 30° to 50°F (-1° to 10°C) in a day.

Kings River Falls is a popular hiking spot in the Ozark Mountains.

Some people vacation in Mount Magazine State Park. At 2,753 feet (839 m), Magazine Mountain is the highest point in Arkansas.

# EARNING A LIVING

Arkansas is a service and manufacturing state. Food is **processed** here. Mining, department stores, and trucking companies are important businesses in the state. They provide jobs.

Arkansas is also known for farming. There is rich soil near the Mississippi River. This area is sometimes called "the Delta." Most of the state's major crops grow there. These include rice, soybeans, and wheat.

**Did You Know?**

The only active US diamond mine is in southeast Arkansas.

Oil, coal, and natural gas are important natural resources found in Arkansas.

# Natural Wonder

The Ozark Mountains are in northwest Arkansas. They include **rugged** land and thick forests. Peaks and valleys were formed by rivers cutting through rock over many years.

Water is a common feature in the Ozarks. The mountains are known for natural springs. Water bubbles up from the ground and forms large pools.

### Did You Know?

Some of the first people in Arkansas lived in the Ozarks. They made homes in caves and under cliffs.

Blanchard Springs (*above*) pours into Mirror Lake. People fish for trout in the lake.

21

# Hometown Heroes

Many famous people are from Arkansas. William Jefferson "Bill" Clinton was born in Hope in 1946. In 1953, his family moved to Hot Springs.

Clinton became one of the country's youngest governors and presidents. He was governor of Arkansas from 1979 to 1981 and again from 1983 to 1992. He was president of the United States from 1993 to 2001.

Clinton continued to be active in politics after serving as president.

23

Maya Angelou was born in 1928 in Saint Louis, Missouri. She grew up in Stamps, Arkansas.

Angelou is a famous author and actress. She acted on television in *Roots*. And, she wrote a book about her childhood in Arkansas. It is called *I Know Why the Caged Bird Sings*.

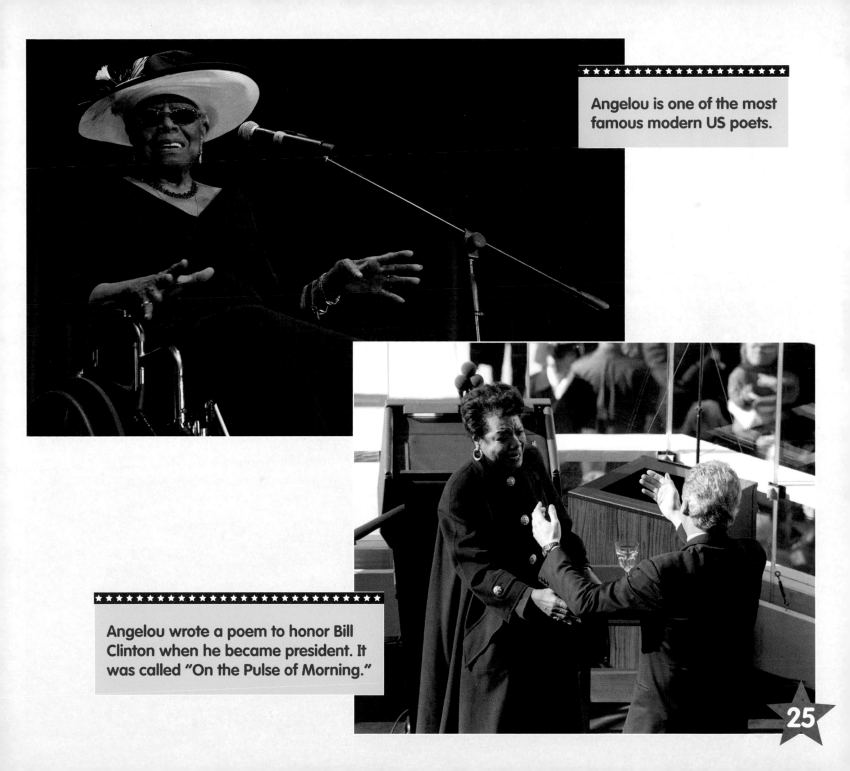

Angelou is one of the most famous modern US poets.

Angelou wrote a poem to honor Bill Clinton when he became president. It was called "On the Pulse of Morning."

25

# Tour Book

Do you want to go to Arkansas? If you visit the state, here are some places to go and things to do!

 ## Taste

Eat rice from the Delta. Arkansas is the number-one grower of rice in the United States.

 ## Heal

Hot Springs National Park is located in the Ouachita Mountains. Water bubbles up from the earth at about 143°F (62°C)! Some believe bathing in this water helps people feel better.

##  Explore

Visit Blanchard Springs Caverns in the Ozarks. There, see limestone caves and an underground river!

## ★ Listen

Take in some live folk music. The Ozark Mountain area is known for this style of music. It uses instruments such as fiddles and has an old-time feel.

##  Discover

Arkansas is called "the Natural State." That's because it has national forests, a national river, and national parks. It also has more than 50 state parks!

# A GREAT STATE

The story of Arkansas is important to the United States. The people and places that make up this state offer something special to the country. Together with all the states, Arkansas helps make the United States great.

Some people call the Ozarks a US treasure.

29

# Fast Facts

**Date of Statehood:**
June 15, 1836

**Population (rank):**
2,915,918
(32nd most-populated state)

**Total Area (rank):**
53,179 square miles
(27th largest state)

**Motto:**
"Regnat Populus"
(The People Rule)

**Nickname:**
The Natural State

**State Capital:**
Little Rock

**Flag:**

**Flower:** Apple Blossom

**Postal Abbreviation:**
AR

**Tree:** Pine Tree

**Bird:** Northern Mockingbird

# Important Words

**American Civil War**  the war between the Northern and Southern states from 1861 to 1865.

**capital**  a city where government leaders meet.

**diverse**  made up of things that are different from each other.

**Louisiana Purchase**  land the United States purchased from France in 1803. It extended from the Mississippi River to the Rocky Mountains and from Canada through the Gulf of Mexico.

**process**  to change something by taking it through a set of actions.

**region**  a large part of a country that is different from other parts.

**resource**  a supply of something useful or valued.

**rugged**  having an uneven surface.

---

# Web Sites

To learn more about Arkansas, visit ABDO Publishing Company online. Web sites about Arkansas are featured on our Book Links page. These links are routinely monitored and updated to provide the most current information available.

**www.abdopublishing.com**

# Index